IMPROVING READING
AT THE EARLY STAGES OF 5 - 14

IMPROVING READING
AT
THE EARLY STAGES
OF
5 - 14

Member of
Plain English Campaign
committed to
clearer communication

27

PEC

A Report by HM Inspectors of Schools
The Scottish Office Education and Industry Department

Further enquiries about this report should be addressed to:
The Scottish Office Education and Industry Department
H M Inspectors of Schools
3B - 05 Victoria Quay
Edinburgh
EH 6 6 QQ

Tel: (0131) 244 0649

ISBN 0 7480 5854 0

Cover photographs: Creative Photography and The Still Moving Picture Company

CONTENTS

FOREWORD

This report is the second in a series which provides advice aimed at raising attainment in the 5-14 age range. The first report was entitled *Improving Mathematics Education 5-14 (HMI 1997)*. This one is concerned with improving attainment in reading at the early stages of 5-14.

In the foreword to *Improving Mathematics Education 5-14*, I invited teachers and others to consider the implications for other areas of the curriculum of that report's messages about the importance of high expectations and an emphasis on achievement. This report continues that theme. It acknowledges that socio-economic factors influence reading standards but confirms that inspections show that there are schools in areas of social disadvantage which achieve excellent standards in reading.

Schools can make a difference - particularly schools which have high expectations, effective teaching and a whole-school approach to reading. Recent advice on the curriculum for the pre-school year will give a better foundation for schools to build on when children enter P1. All headteachers should promote an ethos of achievement in their school, set demanding targets for the school as a whole and for each reading group and develop a consistent approach to reading; and involve parents.

The importance of making early, sustained progress in reading is unchallengeable. Certainly, all aspects of the curriculum are important but the ability to read is an essential preliminary to progress in other areas of learning. If difficulties emerge, they must be identified and attended to immediately. In recent years, a number of projects aimed at improving early reading, especially in areas of social disadvantage, have been introduced by education authorities and the Government is funding intervention initiatives in every education authority. This report complements these initiatives by describing good practice in developing reading at the early stages. It points towards many factors which contribute to successful reading as well as highlighting aspects which are of central importance to effective provision for reading.

The report is based on two principal sources of evidence. The first is HM Inspectorate's national database of evidence from 260 primary schools inspected between 1992 and 1995 which led to the publication of *Standards and Quality in Scottish Schools 1992-95*. This evidence enables the report to comment with confidence on current strengths and weaknesses in teaching reading in primary schools. Secondly, HM Inspectors inspected reading at the early stages in 23 primary schools across Scotland between April 1995 and March 1996 to supplement this national database.

This report should be used by all schools to review their practice in order to improve standards of reading, by education authorities to ensure quality within their schools and by those involved in the pre-service and in-service education of teachers. The report includes a summary intended to help schools to use it for staff development purposes.

DOUGLAS A OSLER
HM Senior Chief Inspector of Schools

1 IMPROVING ATTAINMENT

1.1 The starting points for children beginning to learn to read, in terms of their experience of stories, rhymes, text and language structures can be very different. Many Scottish children enter school with a sound experience of books and print and a tradition of enjoying stories and rhymes at home. This leaves them well motivated towards reading. Some children's early experience of literacy, however, is more limited and the lack of such preparatory experiences slows their progress. This can affect teachers' expectations of them and response to them as learners. Differences in children's experience of reading out of school may continue to affect their progress. Teachers need to take this into account in building on children's prior learning

1.2 The evidence from the national database for 1992-5 indicated that, in five out of six primary schools, almost all of the pupils had achieved Level A in reading by the end of P3. In these schools, good progress had been made to help pupils to achieve an initial competence in reading. In order to attain Level A, pupils must be able to read short straightforward texts and show some understanding of their reading; show evidence of reading for enjoyment and find simple information; and recognise obvious differences between distinct types of text such as a story and a list of instructions. At this stage, most are also beginning to read with greater fluency and convey meaning through their oral expression.

How do you monitor reading standards in your school? What proportion of pupils achieve level A by the end of Primary 3?

1.3 In the one in six schools where reading standards were lower, up to half of the children had not attained Level A by the end of P3. In a few schools the proportion not attaining Level A in P3 was more than half. Such readers remained hesitant and read each word slowly. Where there were large numbers of pupils making slow progress teachers were faced with a considerable challenge. Some regarded this situation with resignation, associating low standards inevitably with problems of deprivation. This view often led to low expectations of pupils, which in turn adversely affected the quality of teaching.

In what ways do you ensure that teachers' expectations are high in your school?

1.4 There is clear evidence from a variety of sources that socio-economic factors do influence reading standards. HM Inspectorate's national database of the 260 primary schools with reports published between 1992 and 1995 shows a statistically significant correlation between reading standards in relation to national attainment targets and socio-economic indicators. The proportion of schools with fair or unsatisfactory standards was higher in areas of social disadvantage than in the set of schools as a whole. This partly reflects the influence of factors outwith the school on reading.

1.5 In contrast, there were some schools in areas of social disadvantage in the national sample which achieved very good standards in reading. For example, four of the schools which had high indicators of social disadvantage achieved very good standards in reading - that is they achieved overall standards which were above those set out in national attainment targets. These schools provide convincing evidence of what can be achieved with high expectations, effective teaching and a whole school approach to reading. Another 25 of the 46 schools which had high indicators of social disadvantage and low indicators of advantage achieved good reading standards.

1.6 The sample also contained one school with low indicators of social disadvantage where overall standards were below those set out in national attainment targets despite a very favourable catchment area. Schools with similar catchments had very different results. The work of individual schools can make a very considerable difference. This makes it particularly important to provide the highest quality of provision and set high expectations in schools where some pupils have limited experience of early literacy.

1.7 In the sample of schools inspected for early reading, most pupils made a good start to reading during the P1 and P2 stages. They generally enjoyed reading aloud and were enthusiastic about books read to them by their teachers. Pupils in P1 showed that they were familiar with the layout of books and some conventions such as how to hold a book and follow the text from left to right. By P2, many were beginning to understand simple terms used in talking about their reading such as 'title' or 'poem'. Most in P2 could talk with confidence about what they had heard or read.

1.8 Most pupils could describe a favourite book from the class library. In one school, teachers encouraged pupils to place 'happy face' bookmarks on books they had enjoyed to encourage them to make personal responses to their reading. In some schools, the reading habit was beginning to be established and most of their pupils had wide reading interests. In other schools, there were groups of pupils with more limited experience of literacy. In these schools a significant proportion of pupils reported very little reading outside of school, beyond reading their reading book to parents. Children with poorer language skills often had a range of other disadvantages including less frequent experience of stories, rhymes and books.

1.9 Pupils in P1 and P2 were able to read captions and labels on classroom displays and most could read back words from their personal wordbooks or from stories which they had written or had scribed for them by the teacher. Almost all could read prepared passages from their reading books with accuracy and understanding. Most could recognise words from the basic vocabulary used in their reading books. By P2, abler readers were reading with greater fluency and could recognise words and parts of words quickly and accurately - an essential skill for successful reading.

1.10   Pupils in the schools inspected for early reading generally made good progress in learning to read unfamiliar words, that is in developing their skills in 'decoding' or 'word attack'. Almost all used familiar characters and illustrations in their reading books to help them to guess the meanings of words or phrases. Where it was helpful, teachers drew pupils' attention to clues in illustrations. The particular topic or story also provided clues which were used to prompt their guesses. Many pupils instinctively used the meaning and pattern of the surrounding words to help them to guess words.

1.11   Phonic approaches to teaching reading were well established in almost all of the schools inspected for early reading. Teachers increasingly used pupils' knowledge of phonics as the main way of helping them when they had difficulty with a word. They often paid particular attention to the beginnings of words.   Most pupils at these stages were confident in recognising individual sounds and some blends at the start of words to identify these beginnings. Teachers sometimes used pupils' knowledge of rhyme to help them to guess sounds at the ends of words.

1.12   For many pupils at these stages, tackling unfamiliar words was a joint activity between teacher and pupil. In the process, pupils gradually acquired independence in decoding words. When a pupil hesitated in reading, most teachers achieved an appropriate balance between telling them the word to maintain the flow of reading and helping the pupil to tackle the unfamiliar word. Sometimes teachers or other pupils interjected words as soon as there was any hesitation from the reader when a brief pause might have allowed the pupil to read the word correctly. In other cases, pupils stopped reading completely when they met an unfamiliar word, not seeming to know what to do next.

1.13   Where pupils in P1 and P2 were aware that what they had read aloud did not make sense, they rarely attempted to re-read to correct their mistakes. They seemed unwilling, without encouragement, to return to the text to try to unravel the meaning again. As pupils' confidence in reading increased during P2, more of them were beginning to use punctuation as an aid to reading with meaning.

1.14   Teachers readily identified pupils who required additional support and in most schools provided additional time to hear them read regularly. However, in some schools and classes such pupils received insufficient support. It is crucial to provide support at an early stage whenever there are clear signs of difficulties or delay in reading. This prevents difficulties becoming established and helps the learner to maintain a positive self-image and attitude to reading as well as to make progress in other aspects of the curriculum.

At what stage is additional support for reading provided in your school? What signs do you look for?

1.15   A small minority of pupils (but this proportion was larger in some schools inspected for early reading) made very slow progress in reading during P1 and P2. Their development needs were diverse and required careful assessment. They were often hesitant in reading and in applying their knowledge of sounds or the meaning of the surrounding words to help them to recognise words or understand the text. Some had difficulty in remembering or talking about stories or books read previously. In some cases, their understanding of the meaning of passages was poor. Motivation and interest in reading varied from very strong in some pupils to weak in others.

What evidence do you have about the rate of progress between P2 and P3 in your school?

1.16 In some schools inspected for early reading, the rate of progress between P2 and P3 was slow. Pupils' reading was competent enough to meet the routine demands of classwork. They could read a passage well, answer factual questions about it or find specific information from a reference book, but overall their skills remained at a plateau. Skills in reading for information were often developed at a superficial level. Whereas most of these pupils were aware of some differences between fiction and non-fiction and many became familiar with terms like 'contents' and 'index', they lacked experience in making sense of information texts. In many of these classes, abler readers were also under-challenged.

1.17 Where practice was best, a challenging reading programme stimulated pupils to extend their skills effectively during P3. In these cases, pupils in P3 were beginning to:

Which of these are features of your reading programme towards the end of the early stages?

- read more widely or at greater length, for example in reading short novels;

- read with increased fluency and expression;

- read to find evidence from a passage, to make simple inferences, to discuss the effectiveness of language and to identify main ideas;

- demonstrate their skills in understanding the language and structure of simple information passages such as descriptions, instructions and reports; and

- discuss books and express their own responses in comments and book reviews.

1.18 All headteachers should promote an ethos of achievement in their schools. They should set demanding targets for the school as a whole and for each reading group to achieve at different points in the year as one way of setting high expectations. They should develop a consistent approach to reading provision by reaching an agreed reading policy with their staff.

1.19 They should implement this policy by identifying staff development needs and planning a programme of staff development which meets these needs. They should make effective use of co-operation amongst staff in teaching reading, involving promoted staff, class teachers, additional teachers and nursery nurses. They should monitor progress towards the achievement of targets for reading and celebrate success when these targets are achieved.

> **In schools inspected between 1992 and 1995, the whole-school standards achieved in relation to national attainment targets for reading were:**
>
> > **very good in 20% of schools**
> > **good in 64% of schools**
> > **fair in 15% of schools**
> > **unsatisfactory in 1% of schools**

2 GOOD USE OF ACCOMMODATION AND RESOURCES

Which of these comments would apply to the reading areas in your school?

2.1   In the schools inspected for early reading, almost all classrooms had areas set aside for reading, but their quality varied widely. In most cases these areas were carpeted and furnished with cushions and chairs to allow pupils to read in comfort. Class libraries were usually well organised and supported by attractive displays of fiction and non-fiction books which tempted readers. However, in some classrooms, book corners were untidy, unattractive and uncomfortable with heaps of books placed untidily on shelves and no comfortable place available for reading. In a few classrooms, the small size of reading corners meant that they were too crowded to allow reading to be taught in comfort.

2.2   A peaceful setting assists the concentration which reading demands of young children. A quiet atmosphere for reading was generally achieved in most early stages classrooms. In a few cases, pupils were distracted by the level of noise or minor disturbances caused by the circulation of pupils or noisy activities too close to the reading area.

2.3   Almost all teachers were aware of the importance of print in the classroom environment. They displayed labels and captions or notices such as instructions for the care of a pet. They used these to show pupils that print carries meaning and to consolidate their recognition of familiar words from reading schemes or class topics. They also displayed pupils' writing to show them that they could communicate with their classmates through the written word.   Some teachers used examples of print in the local environment as reading materials. Although print was well displayed in classrooms, there was scope in most cases to use it more effectively by referring to it more frequently when teaching reading.

How is the use of library resources monitored in your school?

2.4   A minority of schools had a library shared by early stages classes. This was often located in an open area or an area between classrooms. It usually contained a wider collection of reference books than was found in class libraries and sometimes contained fiction. In some cases, schools had difficulties in resourcing their libraries and old or damaged books were not replaced. Some early stages classes used the school library, but, even where books were colour-coded to indicate those appropriate for younger pupils, their visits to the library tended to be too infrequent. Good levels of resourcing and careful monitoring of pupils' use of library books are key factors in making effective use of such centralised libraries.

2.5 Written policies for reading sometimes included advice on effective use of classroom accommodation. There were, however, variations within the same school and across schools in the ways that classroom accommodation was used to support reading. The organisation of class libraries and book corners was too often regarded as a matter only for the class teacher. The creation of a classroom environment which supports interest in books and provides quiet and comfortable conditions to develop reading skills is too important to allow for such variation. School management should discuss with teachers the characteristics of good practice and monitor the implementation of these in classrooms.

How does school management in your school ensure a consistent use of classroom accommodation and resources to support reading?

2.6 All of the schools used a reading scheme as a central part of their reading programme. Headteachers gave a high priority to reading resources and all schools were well resourced for this aspect of reading. In relation to resources for all aspects of reading:

- about 15% of the schools inspected for early reading had very good resources;

- another 80% of schools were well resourced;

- only one school was poorly resourced.

2.7 Most schools had a good range of supplementary reading materials and a good stock of books for reading for enjoyment. They invariably had resources to develop phonic skills and materials which supported the development of spelling, handwriting and writing skills. Most had a stock of reading games and big books for shared reading. There were often sets of audio tapes to allow pupils to listen to sounds, stories and rhymes. In some classes, broadcasts were used effectively to support reading and language development. Computers were readily available, although the software used for reading was often limited to programmes which encouraged practice of a narrow set of reading skills. All classes had access to some non-fiction books but provision of these was sometimes poor and it was rare to find a range of information tapes. In most, but not all, schools there were suitable resources for children who were experiencing difficulties in learning to read.

2.8 Teachers also made their own resources to support reading programmes. In many cases, these were very useful. At best, they were well designed to meet the needs of individual pupils or to provide materials which related to the pupils' experience in the local community or family or to current class topics. For example, some teachers made up reading games, recorded stories on tape and prepared overlays for the concept keyboard. They published pupils' work in well presented booklets and

How satisfactory are the different types of resources described in paras 2.6-2.10 in your school?

designed activities which were well tuned to individual pupil's needs for practice or extension of reading skills. Too often, however, teacher prepared materials merely duplicated exercises from commercial workbooks, taking up valuable teachers' time without adding to the range or quality of resources.

2.9 Weaknesses in specific aspects of resourcing for reading were found in a small proportion of schools. These included:

- the use of resources which were worn or dated

- insufficient resources for learning support

- a limited range of tapes of stories, poetry and rhymes and information

- limited class libraries.

2.10 Schools tried hard to improve and update their resources for reading. Library and resource services were used to extend the stock of books. Some librarians provided high quality story sessions either in schools or in the local library, which aroused interest in books. Occasionally, authors were invited to generate interest in books by reading their stories and talking about events and characters with pupils. Book Clubs and Book Fairs were used to acquire new books for reading at home and school and to encourage the reading habit. In a number of schools, substantial funds raised by parents were used to acquire new resources for reading.

3 GOOD READING PROGRAMMES

3.1   All of the teachers in the early reading survey devoted a substantial amount of time to their reading programmes. The time allocated to reading was consistent with national advice. Some schools where headteachers had concerns about reading standards sensibly allocated additional time to reading. They allocated this time by using a high proportion of the 20% flexibility factor available to primary schools for reading.

3.2   Where practice was good, a rich language programme provided a framework which supported the teaching of reading. It created opportunities to extend pupils' spoken language and to link talking, listening, reading and writing closely together. A range of classroom activities was used to promote interest in reading for enjoyment and for practical and imaginative purposes. These included role play, composing individual or group stories, sequencing pictures, recounting news and events, retelling stories, describing characters and places, following instructions and finding information during investigations, games and making models and displays.

3.3   Talking, listening, reading and writing activities were used consciously to reinforce each other in these situations. Specific links between writing, spelling and reading were productive in developing familiarity with letters, the composition of words and their sounds.

3.4   The reading scheme and the systematic development of phonic skills were often key elements in achieving continuity and progression in reading. Almost all teachers used the reading scheme effectively to develop shared themes for classwork, to match the level of texts to pupils' reading attainments and to assist pupils' progress through more difficult texts. Phonics programmes were generally used effectively to guide the introduction of phonic skills and monitor pupils' success in applying these skills. In a few schools, a haphazard variety of reading schemes or methods of teaching reading were used by different teachers. In these instances, a more active involvement by school management was required to establish a coherent programme of study.

Does your school have a coherent programme of study for reading? How far does it ensure a systematic development of phonic skills?

3.5   Teachers provided a variety of reading activities to supplement the reading scheme and provide a broad and balanced reading programme. Most programmes were structured around the strands of *English Language 5-14*. Teachers' priority in using the reading scheme was usually to develop basic decoding skills and to help pupils to acquire competence in reading with fluency and understanding. They also aimed to develop the habit of reading for pleasure through the reading scheme and their wider reading programme. They often placed less emphasis on developing skills in reading for information.

3.6 The reading and telling of stories, poetry and rhyme and the use of information books by the teacher communicated messages about the value and interest of books to pupils. They provided teachers with opportunities to demonstrate their own enjoyment of books as a model for their pupils. In most classes, teachers encouraged pupils to choose books, to browse through them and to read them for enjoyment or information or read them to their classmates.

What steps do you take to encourage pupils to develop the reading habit?

3.7 However, once again the opportunities for this varied within the same school and across schools. For example, in one school:

"In P1, pupils had very good opportunities to read books quietly and to share them with friends, but, in P2, children could only choose books when their programme of work was completed."

The status that teachers gave to reading of this kind by providing time for it and talking with pupils about the books that they were reading was influential in establishing the habit of reading in class.

How do you teach children to understand and use non-fiction texts?

3.8 Pupils had experience of reading information passages in their reading schemes and in reference books in topic studies. In a significant number of schools, this type of reading was a weakness in the reading programme because pupils had insufficient experience of reading non-fiction texts and in particular non-narrative passages. Pupils were less frequently taught to understand and use non-fiction texts than they were taught to comprehend stories or poems. This lack of teaching compounded the difficulties which many pupils found in reading non-fiction passages.

In schools inspected between 1992 and 1995, reading programmes were:

very good in about 18% of schools

good in 69% of schools

fair in 13% of schools

No schools inspected had unsatisfactory programmes for reading

---

4 IMPROVING LEARNING AND TEACHING

4.1   In the schools inspected for early reading, the reading programme was commonly organised into whole-class, group and individual teaching. Whole-class activities included reading stories to the class, discussing "big books" and some phonics teaching. Much of the remaining time for reading was allocated to teaching groups related to pupils' attainments in reading and to individual follow-up to reading activities. Attention was given to individual needs within group teaching and when children were provided with individual reading times.

4.2   Some very good whole-class teaching of reading was observed. For example, in a lively lesson using a "big book", one teacher effectively encouraged pupils to find links between the story and their personal experiences, to predict what would happen as the story progressed, to recall familiar sounds and to analyse unfamiliar words into sounds in order to help them guess the words. Freed from organisational demands, the teacher concentrated on using her teaching skills to good effect. At the other extreme, whole-class teaching was occasionally poor or continued for too long with the result that pupils lost attention.

4.3   Learning to read in attainment groups allowed pupils to share the enjoyment of books and stories and develop their proficiency in reading as a social and co-operative activity. Almost all pupils were well motivated in group reading and interested in the books provided. They usually had opportunities to ask and answer questions, make comments about their responses or talk about their own experiences where these related to the text.

4.4   Individual reading activities generally fell into the categories of follow-up activities or opportunities to browse through books and read them for enjoyment or information. More attention was generally needed to follow-up activities to reading.   At best, they included high quality discussion, writing, displays and friezes. Often, however, they involved undemanding tasks such as copying, colouring-in and completing word searches. Although they sometimes consolidated and practised skills, these activities often bore little relationship to the learning activities which pupils needed to assist their progress in reading.

What kind of follow-up activities do you use? How do they help pupils to progress in reading?

4.5   Teaching reading in attainment groups allowed pupils to progress at an appropriate pace through the reading scheme. Three important factors created the conditions in which effective teaching of reading could take place in groups. These factors were the use of reading materials well matched to pupils' levels of attainment, providing enough time for each pupil in a group, and ensuring that the time spent teaching reading with each group was of high quality, ie. as far as possible free from interruptions.

*How do you check
that abler readers
are sufficiently
challenged by
reading texts?*

4.6   Teachers were well aware of the first factor, the importance of a good match between the difficulty of texts and pupils' current reading levels. Commendably, in almost all cases, pupils had reading books which were well matched to their reading attainments. This important factor in helping pupils to learn to read was well achieved by early stages teachers. The exception was that, in some classes, and particularly by P3, abler readers should have been given more demanding texts than they were reading.

4.7   The second important factor influencing the learning and teaching of reading is the provision of sufficient time for individual support and attention for each pupil when children are heard reading in groups. In the sample inspected, the time provided varied from an average of only 30 seconds per child in some classes to an average of more than four minutes per child in others. Such differences were sometimes found between classes in the same school. This variation is unreasonably wide. The effectiveness of classroom organisation was crucial in influencing the quantity and also the quality of the individual teaching time provided. Schools should ensure that sufficient time is available for support for each pupil.

*How effective is
your classroom
organisation in
providing sufficient
quality teaching
time for reading?
How is this
monitored by school
management?*

4.8   Thirdly, successful classroom organisation allowed teachers to provide sustained periods of teaching time free from interruptions for each attainment group. In this time, teachers could concentrate on the needs of a particular group and engage in an enjoyable discussion of the text. They could focus effectively on direct teaching for particular purposes, for example to develop fluency or comprehension or phonics or improved motivation towards reading. Many early stages teachers managed this very well: this third factor was successfully achieved in about two thirds of the classes inspected for early reading.   Schools should ensure that quality teaching time is provided for each reading group.

4.9   In about a third of classes observed, the teaching of reading in groups was affected by problems of classroom organisation.   Over-complex classroom organisation was one source of difficulty. Where too many groups or too many different tasks were organised, there were often frequent interruptions to teaching. Teachers sometimes hurried through their work with the reading group, hearing each child's reading in a mechanistic fashion with minimal time for support, discussion of meaning or language use, or enjoyment of the story.   Clear procedures on interruptions during reading worked in some classes. In others, a more manageable system of groups was needed to address the root cause of organisational problems.

4.10   The three factors described above create the conditions in which effective teaching of reading can take place. The quality of that teaching is fundamental in maximising children's progress.   All of the teachers inspected in the early reading survey used a variety of approaches to teaching basic skills in reading with fluency and understanding.   The systematic teaching of phonics and 'look-and-say' approaches was supported in a majority of cases by an emphasis on the meaning and enjoyment of the text and an attempt to promote interest in books.

4.11 Where practice in teaching reading was most effective, these approaches were put into practice through a carefully planned blend of specific activities. The activities set out in the table below describe what teachers do when they teach reading. They provide a useful agenda for all schools to review their classroom practice in reading. Schools should review their practice and ensure that reading is taught effectively in every class.

Table 1: When teachers are teaching reading effectively they:

- listen to pupils talking about their experiences of reading

- discuss stories, events and characters and relate these to pupils' own experiences

- explain the context, where this is outwith the pupil's experience

- teach short phonic lessons e.g. emphasising initial letter sounds and recalling or comparing words with similar sounds in the text, looking at the endings of words and finding words which rhyme

- revisit familiar/key words

- introduce new reading vocabulary

- ask pupils to read aloud to others in the group

- explain the meanings of words

- discuss the effectiveness of the language used

- explain some of the features of different types of text, for example of non-fiction or poetry

- encourage pupils to talk about their favourite parts of stories or favourite characters

- ask pupils to read back scribed stories or captions

- use language games and story tapes.

Which of these activities do you use in teaching reading?

*How does school
management
ensure that
reading is
taught in your
school?*

4.12   In a significant minority of group reading lessons, there was little actual teaching of reading of the kind detailed in the table above. Some teachers seemed to expect all of their pupils to learn to read well by being heard reading aloud. Although some children do learn to read apparently effortlessly and with little teaching, many require much more support. This group of teachers needed to place more emphasis on teaching reading and to provide more time for discussing and responding to passages. It is not enough simply to listen to pupils' reading. Education authorities and Teacher Education Institutions should ensure that skills in the teaching of reading are priorities in pre-service and in-service training courses.

4.13   Good teaching implements a variety of approaches in ways which support one another. The language programme supports the reading programme. Strong links are made between reading and writing. There is an emphasis on the meaning and enjoyment of the text. The use of reading for interest, pleasure and practical purposes is actively promoted. Alongside this, a set of words is established and reinforced as a familiar reading vocabulary. Systematic teaching of phonic skills helps pupils to recognise parts of words and whole words quickly and accurately and 'attack' unfamiliar words. Pupils are taught other ways of 'attacking' words such as using clues from the passage's context or meaning.

4.14   As pupils' confidence grows, the emphasis in teaching and learning shifts to developing their fluency and expression, to extending their comprehension, to encouraging them to use their skills in reading for pleasure and discussion of texts and to develop and apply skills in reading for information.

5 EFFECTIVE ASSESSMENT AND RECORDING OF PUPILS' PROGRESS

5.1 All the teachers assessed pupils as they heard them read. They praised them and gently corrected some of their errors and helped them to analyse and read words and to unlock the meaning from the text. They accurately assessed how suitable reading books were for pupils' reading abilities. They used this information to intervene effectively where pupils had difficulty, but less frequently to offer more challenge where pupils were capable of it.

5.2 They also made judgements about each pupil's strengths, development needs and progress in reading. These judgements were generally sound, but sometimes missed important aspects of pupils' individual needs or approaches to reading. It was rare for teachers to take notes of their observations and judgements as they were hearing reading. In the best practice, teachers made brief notes of their observations whilst listening to pupils read and used these to take short term action or to build a profile of each pupil's reading attainments.

What are the advantages of making notes as you hear reading? How would you use the information recorded?

5.3 Almost all of the teachers kept careful records of what each individual had read within the reading scheme. Most also used checklists to record the phonic skills covered or mastered by pupils. Some teachers recorded the reading vocabulary which had been introduced to groups or ticked the words readily recognised by individual pupils. Forward plans for reading varied in the extent to which they set out clearly skills or learning experiences in reading, rather than merely indicating the reading resources to be used.

5.4 Some teachers maintained useful records or summaries of pupils' particular strengths and development needs in reading, by writing descriptive comments. For example:

> "One teacher kept excellent, concise records which covered what individuals had read, how they had performed, what specific needs had been noted and how phonic skills were developing."

Such a level of recording was unusual. The majority of teachers recorded the current reading book and more detailed information about phonic skills. They regarded this as a broad summary of each pupil's competence in reading. In addition, they relied on keeping information about pupils' strengths and development needs in their heads.

5.5 Teachers met groups regularly for reading and most teachers had a good knowledge of their pupils' strengths and development needs. Storing such assessment evidence mentally could be effective where teachers had clear aims for reading and where they acted on their observations quickly in planning teaching related to group and individual needs. However, where aims for reading required clarification, and assessment evidence was not promptly used to modify teaching, then more comprehensive record keeping served a valuable role in developing these aspects of good practice.

How good is your school's approach to record keeping? How manageable and effective is your approach to monitoring pupils' progress?

5.6   There were variations in practice in record keeping within schools as well as across schools. Some schools lacked a common format for record keeping. Others struggled in setting clear expectations about what was a manageable and useful level of detail in record keeping. Where schools had developed over-ambitious records, these had frequently fallen into disuse. Some schools had developed useful records, but teachers still planned the next steps in learning only in terms of the group moving on to the next reading book. Many schools still had some way to go in establishing a manageable, whole-school system of record keeping which influenced teaching. It is clear that for early intervention to be successful and for appropriate support to be provided as pupils move through the school, schools need to keep careful track of pupils' progress in reading. Records should contain a concise summary of assessment evidence and the results of national tests.

5.7   Diagnostic assessment and more systematic record keeping were found more frequently where learning support teachers or promoted staff were involved in supporting individuals or small groups in reading. In these cases, individualised educational programmes based on assessments were usually planned, implemented and reviewed. These programmes often promoted valuable dialogue between teachers about the progress of individual pupils. In turn, this tended to improve the quality of reporting to parents.

How is assessment information used in reviewing individual pupils' progress and grouping pupils for reading in your school?

5.8   Where they were established, periodic reviews of pupils' reading were important in planning the next steps in learning for all pupils and identifying needs for additional support. For example, in one school:

> "Teachers wrote comments about the progress of groups and on some individuals in the 'evaluation' section of their forward plans. There was a very good and regular assessment of every pupil's strengths, needs and next steps in learning to which all relevant staff had access."

This good practice clearly supported the school's intention to intervene early and provide support where there were signs of a lack of progress in reading.

5.9   During P2 or P3, some schools screened pupils for progress in reading or for their general progress in learning. Standardised reading tests were sometimes used as one element in screening. Teachers' assessments of pupils' strengths and development needs also provided evidence for screening. Where assessment practice was effective, this provided the most useful evidence for screening and the earlier that it was established the better. In schools where assessment practice was less well developed, screening tests acted as a useful safety net which led to staff taking a closer look at some pupils' reading development. Evidence from national tests was used to confirm teachers' judgements in most, but not all, of the schools inspected. Psychologists, learning support teachers or promoted staff were sometimes involved in screening and with the valuable staff development associated with it.

5.10 Periodic reviews of reading progress were also important in considering whether changes were required to reading groups because some pupils' attainments had become markedly different from those of the rest of the group. Some teachers did adjust reading groups on the basis of assessment evidence, sometimes with the involvement of promoted staff. In other classes, reading groups unfortunately remained unchanged irrespective of variations in progress. Schools should ensure that the allocation of pupils to reading groups is kept under review.

5.11 Where assessment and record keeping were sound, evidence for reporting to parents was readily available. In many of the schools inspected for early reading, education authority formats for reporting were being used. These followed national advice and encouraged descriptive comments on strengths and development needs. Where teachers kept insufficient records, they had a more difficult task in formulating comments for reports. Some schools had more regular methods of reporting to parents about reading. For example, many teachers, particularly those in P1, exchanged information informally with parents at the beginning or end of the school day. Parent-teacher diaries or homework jotters were also used in some schools to encourage exchange of comments about reading.

5.12 All of the schools had arrangements to pass on information from teacher to teacher. Written information typically consisted of a list of pupils in each reading group with a record of books read in the reading scheme and a phonics record. As indicated in paragraph 5.4, it was unusual for teachers to maintain written records of pupils' strengths and development needs. This meant that oral communication was important in passing information to the next teacher. In some schools, arrangements for this were sound with a dedicated time for teachers to transfer information to the teacher at the next stage. In others, there was too much reliance on passing information informally between teachers.

What arrange-
ments are made
in your school to:

• *pass information*
on reading from
teacher to teacher

• *obtain inform-*
ation about
children's pre-
school literacy
experiences?

5.13 In a small minority of schools, language profiles on individual children were passed from the nursery school to primary teachers. These provided teachers with very useful information on children's early experience of language and literacy and on children who needed particular support. Unfortunately, there were instances where these profiles were passed to parents but not to primary schools or where, having reached primary schools, they did not reach all appropriate teachers.

5.14   Sound assessment evidence assisted headteachers in some schools to monitor reading standards.   It informed their judgements about where standards were good as well as where groups of pupils were making insufficient progress and improvements were required.   Assessments of attainment levels confirmed by national tests provided useful evidence about standards achieved towards the end of P3, a key indicator of the success of early stages provision.   For purposes of early intervention, however, such data comes too late. Headteachers should therefore use other methods to monitor standards from P1 onwards and identify children needing support.   Sound assessment evidence, baseline assessments, standardised tests and the levels in a reading scheme reached by groups can all contribute in this respect. Schools, education authorities and HMI should work together to provide advice on baseline assessment.

6 IMPROVING SUPPORT FOR LEARNING TO READ

6.1   In almost all of the schools inspected for early reading there were learning support teachers or other teachers assigned to learning support roles. These teachers almost always had some contact with early stages classes, although in some schools their work did not begin until P3. A tradition had developed in many schools of not using learning support staff in P1 or P2 classes. This was partly because the gap between some pupils' attainments and those of their classmates was more marked at later stages. It was also to allow time for children to settle into school and for initial learning difficulties to be resolved through day to day teaching and learning in P1 and P2.

6.2   Several schools had recently departed from this tradition. In the schools visited, there was a noticeable shift in practice towards the deployment of additional staff, including learning support staff, in P1 and P2. The arguments for such early intervention are powerful. It is important to create the best conditions for successful learning as early as possible. It is unwise to allow a pattern of unsuccessful learning to develop and persist over two important years of primary education before providing additional support in P3. It is important to provide early success in reading to maintain pupils' motivation, self-esteem and positive attitudes to reading. This shift in practice was therefore very welcome. Schools should provide support for learning at an early stage before difficulties become established.

What is your policy for deploying learning support staff? How do they support reading at the early stages?

6.3   The schools inspected used different models of deploying learning support staff. In some schools, their deployment was aimed at all children within the class by improving the time and individual attention available or by enriching the curriculum or providing more opportunities for active learning. Within this model, the learning support teacher and class teacher might each take responsibility for a group of children over a period of time or might rotate among different groups within the class. Although this model of learning support was designed to support all of the children, the availability of two teachers also provided more support for individuals with particular needs.

6.4   In other schools, deployment of learning support teachers was targeted at a small group of pupils, usually those who were experiencing difficulties in learning to read. In this model, the argument was that resources were concentrated where they were most needed.

6.5   Both of these models have merit in particular circumstances. In some schools they were combined very effectively to provide learning support.

The former improved the quality of day to day learning and teaching and allowed for more effective differentiation and targeting of attention in an unobtrusive way. The latter provided concentrated and highly focused diagnosis and support for children with persistent difficulties in learning to read.

*How consistent
is learning
support practice
in your school
in:*

· • *arrangements
for liaison;*

• *identifying
needs for
support;*

• *planning
suitable
programmes;*

• *learning and
teaching
approaches;*

• *assessment
and record
keeping;*

• *reviewing
pupils'
progress?*

6.6 Learning support staff adopted a variety of roles in working with teachers and pupils. Some time was spent in observing children working on a range of activities to assess their needs and approaches to learning. In some schools, learning support teachers played a leading role in diagnostic assessment and in recording and reviewing progress of pupils with particular needs. They acted as consultants to class teachers, providing advice about appropriate plans or resources for individuals or small groups of pupils.

6.7 Often a member of the management team had responsibility for co-ordinating learning support. For example, in one school an assistant headteacher had a remit to: co-ordinate communication between teacher/pupil/parents/ headteacher/outside agencies; provide advice to class teachers and work in consultation with them in drawing up individualised educational programmes for pupils; work alongside class teachers; and monitor pupils' progress.

Whether it was a learning support teacher, an assistant headteacher or the headteacher who had such responsibilities, co-ordination and consistency in the work of all those involved in learning support was essential to its effectiveness.

6.8 Pupils requiring learning support were usually first identified by class teachers' assessments of their progress. This was followed by learning support teachers or promoted staff taking a closer look at their needs. This sometimes involved observation of the pupil in the class and consideration of a range of assessment evidence. In one school, for example:

> "Procedures for identifying difficulties were well established and included consideration of nursery profiles and diagnostic assessment by teachers and the assistant headteacher. Thereafter, progress was carefully monitored."

Less frequently, screening or testing started the process of taking a closer look at a pupil's needs for support. It was good practice for parents to be consulted at an early stage and to be involved in supporting their child's learning as fully as possible. Where specific difficulties are identified, specialist help should be provided and individualised educational programmes (as described in paragraph 5.7) are needed.

6.9 When learning support staff were involved, assessment, recording and monitoring of pupils' progress often became more systematic. It was more common to find records of pupils' strengths and development needs and plans which indicated their next steps in learning. It was also more common to find that assessment evidence was updated by checking that previous skills were maintained.

6.10 There were wide variations among learning support teachers in the breadth of their approach where pupils had experienced difficulties in learning to read. Some adopted a broad approach. They stimulated interest and motivation and positive attitudes towards reading by using fresh resources which were parallel in difficulty to those of the reading scheme and by widening their pupils' experience of enjoyable stories and rhymes. Many fostered spoken language development, using talking and listening activities to develop wider skills which support reading development. Activities drawn from other curriculum areas such as art and design, music or drama were sometimes employed as well as spelling, handwriting or writing.

6.11 Other teachers focused very directly on a subset of reading skills. These teachers concentrated on word recognition, phonic skills, hearing reading and simple comprehension. Their work mirrored many aspects of the reading programme in class. For some pupils, a focused programme met their needs for individual attention, for practice, for more systematic development of phonics, and for more frequent and extended opportunities to read. For others, it was a repetition of aspects of learning with which they had been unsuccessful, where 'more of the same' reinforced their sense of failure. For these pupils, a change of approach was required. The most effective practice matched the approach and programme to a sound assessment of the needs of individuals or small groups of pupils. It provided explicit and systematic phonics teaching but also took account of a variety of learning strengths and development needs which included attitudes and motivation, oral and written language development and the development of comprehension and fluency.

6.12 Arrangements for liaison between learning support teachers, class teachers and promoted staff were generally good. Most of the schools inspected had recognised the importance of good communication about programmes and the progress of individual pupils by dedicating regular times to planning and discussion. For example, in one school:

> "The learning support teacher met class teachers formally every two weeks to discuss provision for individual pupils and, in addition, they all met as a group for planning purposes at the start of each term."

In contrast, some schools still relied on very limited opportunities for informal discussion among teachers.

6.13 All of the schools inspected had a range of contacts with external services. In a number of them, psychological services and area learning support staff were supporting early intervention in reading by providing advice and in-service training to teachers based on current research in reading. In some schools, children's needs for speech and language therapy were not being met because of the limited availability of speech and language therapists. This not only affected pupils' confidence and progress in spoken language but also impeded specific aspects of skill development which are applied in reading.

7 CLOSER PARTNERSHIP WITH PARENTS

7.1   Parents prepare children for reading long before they start school, for example, by providing a varied experience of spoken language, by reading stories and rhymes, labels and signs to their children, by encouraging them to look at pictures and books. Most parents continue to help their children to learn to read once they start school by hearing reading at home. By making time to read with their children and hear them read, parents show their children the value that they place on reading and motivate them to read well. In practical terms, they also provide a considerable increase in the time which children spend in reading aloud in comparison with the brief periods available in school.

7. 2   Schools should make clear to parents the value that they place on parents' contribution to children's success in reading and help them to develop their role in supporting their child's reading.   Pre-school education has an important contribution in establishing patterns of partnership which can be consolidated in primary schools.   However, within the schools inspected for early reading, there was wide variation in the quality of the arrangements to prepare parents to help their children to learn to read.

7.3   Almost all of the schools inspected held meetings to explain to parents their methods of teaching reading and to discuss their role in supporting their children's reading. Schools usually responded sensitively where parents themselves experienced difficulty in reading.   In some schools, information about reading was included within a more general meeting about the curriculum or the life of the school. This was unlikely to provide sufficient   information or support to parents in helping their children with reading at home. All schools should have sound arrangements to explain their approach to reading to parents and involve them in supporting their children's reading.

7.4   In a majority of schools one or more meetings was held specifically on the topic of reading. These arrangements were much more likely to meet parents' needs for support in helping their children to learn to read. Sometimes meetings were arranged before children started school and picture books were provided for parents and children to enjoy at home. Meetings were continued into the first year of school at the point when parents were becoming involved regularly with reading at home.   These were sometimes organised for small groups of parents and sometimes for the whole year group.

What kind of meetings or work-shops are held in your school to support parents in helping their children with reading at home?

7.5 In the best practice, these sessions highlighted the importance of a positive experience of reading for child and parent as well as providing advice on helping children to learn to read. In some cases, they were usefully associated with initiatives in paired or shared reading. Commendably, they sometimes provided opportunities to observe teachers working on reading with groups of pupils so that parents could observe the range of strategies used.

How good is written material for parents in your school?

7.6 In about half of the schools inspected, written materials were provided for parents. These were principally intended to reinforce advice provided at meetings or workshops, but also encouraged interest in reading activities such as book fairs or visits to the local library. At their best, they were well presented, clearly written and provided helpful advice in a way which was accessible to all parents. Sometimes they were written in an inaccessible style and poorly designed and illustrated, which defeated their purpose.

7.7 Parental response to meetings about reading also varied. There was almost always a very good response where children were preparing to start school or where meetings were held early in Primary 1. A particularly good response was reported where parents were invited to the school in small groups, perhaps because the invitation was more personal. After P1, interest sometimes waned and attendance was reduced, for example:

> "The meetings only attracted one in three parents despite the fact that they were held both in the afternoon and the evening."

This underlines the importance of using the early peak of parental interest to communicate messages to parents about reading. It also suggests that small group invitations may be more effective in sustaining parental involvement throughout the early stages.

How effective are your arrangements for continuing support for parental involvement in reading?

7.8 In some schools, the advice provided at meetings was supplemented by continuing arrangements for support. Some schools used two-way diaries, notebooks or cards for teachers and parents to exchange day to day comments about children's reading at home and school. Sometimes helpful instructions were provided which defined particular parental roles in supporting the child, for example "I will read to you," or "Please, read this story with me," or "Please read this to me and ask me questions." Others used comments to indicate where reading had been successful or where help was required. In some schools, class teachers or a promoted member of staff made time available at the end of a day for parents who needed advice on reading. Schools should review their practice to determine the best ways that they can support parents in helping their children to learn to read.

7.9 Support for parents was most effective and highly valued by parents where meetings, written information and continuing support was provided. However, the organisational demands on staff and staff time were considerable. In some cases, parental involvement in the process was difficult to sustain. Where priority had not been given to supporting parents, their involvement in exchanging comments or seeking out specific help quickly waned. Where schools decide to extend the role of parental involvement in reading, they must also be prepared to invest the time, energy and skills required to make it work.

How high a priority is placed on parental involvement in reading in your school?

7.10 As a result of all of these differences, parents in some schools are in a good position to support their children's reading. Other schools do not work sufficiently closely with parents to achieve this level of confidence and support. This is a matter of concern in the light of evidence from research and inspection of the significant differences that parental support can make to attainment in reading. These gains depend on parents establishing a confident and supportive relationship with their children during reading and knowing how to respond when children need help.

8 AGENDA FOR ACTION

8.1   The central importance of reading in pupils' learning is widely accepted by parents, teachers and the general public. They can be assured that reading standards in primary schools are generally good. Most pupils learn to read easily and well. However, in one in six schools, reading standards are too low and there is no evidence that reading standards have improved during recent decades.

8.2   A proportion of pupils continue to leave primary schools with unsatisfactory competence in reading. In some schools, almost half of the pupils lag two or more years behind average attainment in reading. This represents an unnecessary loss of potential. It has serious effects on pupils' education and their futures because reading is a core skill, essential to the acquisition of a range of other learning skills.

8.3   This report has identified a number of key factors which affect standards of attainment in reading and which should be addressed by all schools. The factors listed in the table below provide a clear agenda for raising standards.

Table 2: Key factors in raising reading standards:

- high expectations for all pupils

- good, well organised teaching of reading

- careful assessment of pupils' progress and reading standards

- effective support for pupils where they have particular needs in reading

- a consistent and effective whole-school approach, led and supported by management

- effective involvement of parents in supporting children's progress in reading

8.4   Key Recommendations

These are grouped under the key factors in raising reading standards identified in the Agenda for Action.

high expectations for all pupils

- Schools should promote an ethos of high achievement in reading (1.18).

- They should set demanding targets for the school as a whole and for each reading group in each class to achieve as one way of raising expectations (1.18).

- They should monitor progress towards these targets carefully (1.19).

good, well organised teaching of reading

- Schools should ensure that reading materials are well matched to pupils' reading levels and to their needs to develop skills in reading for enjoyment and reading for information (3.8; 4.6).

- Schools should ensure that sufficient time is available for support for each pupil (4.7).

- Schools should ensure that quality teaching time, ie. time free from interruptions is provided for each reading group (4.8).

- Schools should review their practice and ensure that reading is taught effectively in every class (4.11).

- Education authorities and Teacher Education Institutions should ensure that skills in the teaching of reading are treated as priorities in pre-service and in-service training courses (4.12).

careful assessment of pupils' progress and reading standards

- Schools should keep careful track of pupils' progress in reading using assessment evidence and national tests (5.6).

- They should ensure that the allocation of pupils to reading groups is kept under review (5.10).

- They should monitor reading standards from P1 onwards and identify pupils needing additional support (5.14).

- Schools, education authorities and HMI should work together to provide advice on baseline assessment (5.14).

effective support for pupils where they have particular needs in reading

- Schools should provide support for learning to read at an early stage before difficulties become established (6.2).

- They should ensure that sound assessment evidence is used in identifying, diagnosing and monitoring pupils' progress (6.8 - 6.9).

- They should ensure that the approaches used are carefully matched to the needs of individuals or small groups of pupils (6.11).

a consistent and effective whole-school approach, led and supported by management

- Every school should have a policy for reading which achieves a clear, shared understanding by staff on:
    - the use of accommodation and resources (2.5);
    - the reading programme (3.4; 3.7);
    - teaching and learning approaches (4.10);
    - assessment and recording (5.6);
    - the involvement of parents (7.3; 7.6; 7.8); and
    - the role of learning support and other staff (6.3).

- School management should support the implementation of a school reading policy by:
    - identifying staff development needs;
    - organising staff development ;
    - careful planning of co-operative teaching;
    - monitoring classroom practice; and
    - monitoring pupils' progress in reading (1.19).

effective involvement of parents in supporting children's progress in reading

- Schools should implement their policy on parental involvement in reading by:

    - explaining to parents the school's approaches to teaching reading (7.3); and

    - supporting parents in helping their children to learn to read (7.8).

STAFF DEVELOPMENT SUMMARY

REVIEWING AND DEVELOPING READING PROVISION

This summary is designed to assist schools in reviewing and developing their provision for reading. It contains the series of staff development questions which were raised alongside the text and a summary of the strengths and weaknesses in provision described in the report.

Staff development questions

Improving attainment

How are reading standards monitored in your school?

At what stage is additional support provided for pupils?

What signs do you look for in allocating support?

What evidence do you have about pupils' rate of progress between each stage at P1-P3?

What proportion of pupils achieve Level A by the end of P3?

In what ways do you ensure that teachers' expectations are high in your school?

Are targets set for each reading group to achieve at different points in the year?

Is progress towards these targets monitored?

Good use of accommodation and resources

Are the reading areas in your school

- well organised with attractive displays of books or

- untidy, unattractive and uncomfortable?

How does school management ensure a consistent use of accommodation and resources for reading?

How is the use of library resources monitored?

How satisfactory are the resources for reading in terms of your:

- reading scheme;

- supplementary reading materials;

- books for reading for enjoyment and information; and

- resources for 'follow-up' activities?

Good reading programmes

Does your school have a clear programme of study for reading?

How far does it ensure a systematic development of phonic skills?

What steps do you take to encourage pupils to develop the reading habit?

How do you teach children to understand and use non-fiction texts?

Improving learning and teaching

How do you ensure that texts are matched to pupils' reading attainments and that abler pupils are sufficiently challenged by texts?

How do 'follow-up' activities support the learning which pupils need in order to make progress in reading?

How effective is your classroom organisation in providing sufficient quality teaching time for reading? How is this monitored by management?

Which activities do you use in **teaching** reading?

How does school management ensure that reading is **taught** (rather than listened to) in your school?

Effective assessment and recording of pupils' progress

What are the advantages of making notes as you hear reading? How would you use the information recorded?

How good is your school's approach to record keeping? How manageable and effective is your approach in monitoring pupils' progress?

How is assessment information used in reviewing individual pupil's progress and grouping pupils for reading?

What arrangements are made to:

- pass information on reading from teacher to teacher

- obtain information about children's pre-school literacy experience?

Improving support for learning to read

What is your policy for deploying learning support staff at the early stages? How effective is this deployment?

How consistent is learning support practice in your school in:

- arrangements for liaison

- identifying needs for support

- planning suitable programmes

- assessment and record keeping

- reviewing pupils' progress?

Closer partnership with parents

How high a priority is placed on parental involvement in your school?

What kinds of meetings or workshops are held in your school to support parents in helping their children with reading at home?

How good is written material for parents in your school?

How effective are arrangements for continuing support for parental involvement in reading?

SUMMARY OF STRENGTHS AND WEAKNESSES
IN READING PROVISION

Improving attainment

Strengths

In five out of six schools in
Scotland, almost all of the pupils
had achieved Level A in reading by
the end of P3.

Most pupils in the schools
inspected for early reading made a
good start to reading during P1
and P2. They generally enjoyed
reading aloud and were
enthusiastic about the books read
to them by their teachers.

They generally made good
progress in learning to read
unfamiliar words. They were
beginning to use phonic
approaches.

Teachers readily identified pupils
who required more support and in
most schools provided additional
time to hear them read regularly.

Weaknesses

In schools where reading standards
were lower (one in six schools), up
to half of the children had not
attained Level A by the end of P3.
In a few schools this proportion
was more than half. Some teachers
had low expectations of their
pupils which influenced the quality
of teaching.

A small minority of pupils made
very slow progress in reading
during P1 and P2 in the schools
inspected for early reading. This
proportion was larger in some
schools.

In some schools and classes pupils
requiring additional help received
insufficient support at an early
stage.

The rate of progress between P2
and P3 was slow in some schools
inspected.

SUMMARY OF STRENGTHS AND WEAKNESSES IN READING PROVISION

Good use of accommodation and resources

Strengths	*Weaknesses*
Class libraries were usually well organised and supported by attractive displays of fiction books which tempted readers.	In some classrooms, book corners were untidy, unattractive and uncomfortable with heaps of books placed untidily on shelves and no place available for comfortable reading.
A quiet atmosphere for reading was generally achieved in early stages classrooms.	In a few cases, reading groups were distracted by the level of noise.
Print was usually well displayed in classrooms.	There was scope to use displays of print more effectively by referring to it more frequently in teaching reading.
Headteachers gave a high priority to reading resources and 95% of the schools inspected had good or better levels of resourcing for reading.	There were variations within the same school and across schools in the use of the classroom accommodation to support reading.

SUMMARY OF STRENGTHS AND WEAKNESSES
IN READING PROVISION

Good reading programmes

Strengths	*Weaknesses*
All of the teachers in the early reading survey allocated time to reading which was consistent with national advice.	
Reading programmes were good or better in about 87% of schools in Scotland.	In a significant number of schools, reading for information was a weakness in the reading programme.
Almost all teachers used the reading scheme effectively to match the level of texts to pupils' reading attainments.	In a few schools, a haphazard variety of reading schemes or methods of teaching reading was used by different teachers.
Phonics programmes were generally used effectively to guide the introduction of phonic skills and monitor pupils' success in applying these skills.	
In most classes inspected, teachers encouraged pupils to choose books, to browse through them and to read them for enjoyment or information.	Opportunities for reading for enjoyment varied within the same school as well as varying among schools.

SUMMARY OF STRENGTHS AND WEAKNESSES
IN READING PROVISION

Improving learning and teaching

Strengths

In almost all cases, pupils had reading books which were well matched to their reading attainments.

In about two-thirds of the classes inspected, successful classroom organisation allowed quality teaching time to be spent with each reading group.

All of the teachers used a variety of approaches to teach skills in reading with fluency and understanding.

Where practice in teaching reading was most effective, reading was taught through a carefully planned blend of specific activities (see table 1).

Weaknesses

In some classes, and particularly by P3, abler readers should have been given more demanding texts.

Too frequently, follow up activities involved undemanding tasks which bore little relationship to the learning activities which pupils needed to assist their progress in reading.

In about a third of classes, the time provided for individual support and attention for each pupil during group reading was adversely affected by problems of classroom organisation.

In a significant minority of group reading lessons, there was little actual teaching of reading. A group of teachers needed to place more emphasis on teaching reading and to provide more time for discussing and responding to passages.

SUMMARY OF STRENGTHS AND WEAKNESSES IN READING PROVISION

Effective assessment and recording of pupils' progress

Strengths

Teachers generally made sound judgements about each pupil's strengths, development needs and progress in reading.

Almost all of the teachers kept careful records of what each individual had read within the reading scheme. Most also used checklists to record the phonic skills covered or mastered by pupils.

Where they were established, periodic reviews of pupils' reading were important in planning the next steps in learning for all pupils and identifying needs for additional support.

Evidence from national tests was used to confirm teachers' judgements in most of the schools inspected.

All of the schools had arrangements to pass on information from teacher to teacher.

Weaknesses

Teachers' judgements sometimes missed important aspects of pupils' individual needs or approaches to reading.

It was rare for teachers to take notes of their observations and judgements as they were hearing reading.

Many schools still had some way to go in establishing a manageable whole-school system of record keeping which influenced teaching.

In some schools, there was too much reliance on informal arrangements for transferring information about pupils' strengths and development needs.

SUMMARY OF STRENGTHS AND WEAKNESSES IN READING PROVISION

Improving support for learning to read

Strengths	*Weaknesses*
In some schools, effective learning support provision allowed for more effective differentiation and targeting of attention and provided highly focused diagnosis and support for pupils.	
When learning support staff were involved, assessment and recording and monitoring of pupils' progress often became more systematic.	
Arrangements for liaison between learning support teachers, class teachers and promoted staff were generally good.	Some schools still relied on very limited opportunities for informal discussion among teachers.
	In some schools children's needs for speech and language therapy were not being met because of the limited availability of speech and language therapists.

SUMMARY OF STRENGTHS AND WEAKNESSES IN READING PROVISION

Closer partnership with parents

Strengths

Almost all of the schools inspected held meetings to explain to parents their methods of teaching reading and to discuss the role of parents in supporting reading. In about half of the schools, written advice was also provided.

In some schools, the advice provided at meetings was supplemented by continuing arrangements for support.

Support for parents was most effective and highly valued by parents where meetings, written information and continuing support was provided.

Weaknesses

In some schools, there were no meetings devoted to reading and no written advice to support parents in helping their children with reading at home.

In some cases, parental involvement in the process was difficult to sustain. Where priority had not been given to supporting parents, their involvement in exchanging comments or seeking out help quickly waned.

Printed in the UK for The Stationery Office
J40164, C150, 03/98, CCN 010251